WHAT CHRISTMAS IS
AS
WE GROW OLDER

BY
CHARLES DICKENS

PRIVATELY PRINTED
BY
SMITH & PORTER PRESS
BOSTON
1924

Printing Statement:

Due to the very old age and scarcity of this book,
many of the pages may be hard to read due to the
blurring of the original text, possible missing pages,
missing text and other issues beyond our control.

Because this is such an important and rare work, we
believe it is best to reproduce this book regardless of
its original condition.

Thank you for your understanding.

"I hear along our street
Pass the minstrel throngs;
Hark! they play so sweet,
On their hautboys, Christmas songs!
Let us by the fire
Ever higher
Sing them till the night expire!"

Christmas Eve—that night of candles, of blazing Yule-logs, of minstrelsy
and mirth, of open-hearted hospitality
—yes, and of memories! How deftly,
how tenderly, with what sympathetic
humor Dickens has revealed our hearts'
innermost feelings on this greatest of all
festivals.

Christmas Eve is a three-way time: a
time to pause and look back on the year
that is almost gone; to gaze into the
glimmering fire, and there in the flick-
ering lights and shadows to glimpse

once again dear faces illumined now by celestial radiance, and to feel the friendly pressure of unseen fingers stretching out of the Great Mystery.

It is a time, too, for inner searching, for a re-birth of hope and of consecration to those nobler impulses to which we all would be true.

And it is, in the finest sense, a time for the lightest hearted merry-making. What a hold it has on all our hearts! From earliest English writings come such echoes as

"Christmas comes but once a year:
And when it comes, it brings good cheer."

Going back to the festival of *Juul* of our English forebears, with its flaming *Yule-clog*, its boar's head and huge *candles, Christmas Eve has been ever a time for rejoicing, the "Mother Night" dating from which the days begin to lengthen. Its hearty feasts are the theme of many an ancient carol. Poor Robin's Almanack, 1695, preserves this gem:*

"In the thrice-welcome Christmas, which brings us good cheer,
Minced pies and plum porridge, good ale and strong beer;
With pig, goose and capon, the best that may be,
So well doth the weather and our stomachs agree."

So light the candles, sing the carols, hang the mistletoe, and cry "Ule, ule, ule!" again on Christmas Eve. And then, when stockings are hung, and tousled heads snuggle to happy dreams,

ix

and older folk gather about the quiet hearth, far across the snow we hear the Christmas bells:

"A thousand bells ring out and throw
Their peals abroad, and smite
The darkness, charmed and holy now!
The night that erst no name had worn,
To it a happy name is given;
For in that stable lay, new-born,
The peaceful Prince of earth and
     heaven,
In the solemn midnight
     Centuries ago."

F. ALLEN BURT,
Brookline, 1924.

x

TIME was, with most of us, when Christmas Day, encircling all our limited world like a magic ring, left nothing out for us to miss or seek; bound together all our home enjoyments, affections, and hopes; grouped everything and every one around the Christmas fire; and made the little picture shining in our bright eyes, complete.

Time came, perhaps, all so soon! when our thoughts overleaped that narrow boundary; when there was some one (very dear, we thought then, very beautiful, and absolutely perfect) wanting to the fulness of our happiness; when we were want-

1

ing too (or we thought so, which did just as well) at the Christmas hearth by which that some one sat; and when we intertwined with every wreath and garland of our life that some one's name.

That was the time for the bright visionary Christmases which have long arisen from us to show faintly, after summer rain, in the palest edges of the rainbow! That was the time for the beatified enjoyment of the things that were to be, and never were, and yet the things that were so real in our resolute hope that it would be hard to say, now, what realities achieved since, have been stronger!

2

What! Did that Christmas never really come when we and the priceless pearl who was our young choice were received, after the happiest of totally impossible marriages, by the two united families previously at daggers-drawn on our account? When brothers and sisters in law who had always been cool to us before our relationship was effected, perfectly doted on us, and when fathers and mothers overwhelmed us with unlimited incomes?

Was that Christmas dinner never really eaten, after which we arose, and generously and eloquently rendered honour to our late rival, pres-

3

ent in the company, then and there exchanging friendship and forgiveness, and founding an attachment, not to be surpassed in Greek or Roman story, which subsisted until death? Has that same rival long ceased to care for that same priceless pearl, and married for money, and become usurious? Above all, do we really know, now, that we should probably have been miserable if we had won and worn the pearl, and that we are better without her?

That Christmas when we had recently achieved so much fame; when we had been carried in triumph somewhere, for doing something

4

great and good; when we had won
an honoured and ennobled name,
and arrived and were received at
home in a shower of tears of joy;
—is it possible that *that* Christmas
has not come yet?

And is our life here, at the best,
so constituted that, pausing as we
advance at such a noticeable mile-
stone in the track as this great birthday, we look back on the things
that never were, as naturally and full
as gravely as on the things that have
been and are gone, or have been and
still are? If it be so, and so it seems
to be, must we come to the con-
clusion that life is little better than

a dream, and little worth the loves and strivings that we crowd into it?

No! Far be such miscalled philosophy from us, dear Reader, on Christmas Day! Nearer and closer to our hearts be the Christmas spirit, which is the spirit of active usefulness, perseverance, cheerful discharge of duty, kindness and forbearance! It is in the last virtues especially, that we are, or should be, strengthened by the unaccomplished visions of our youth; for, who shall say that they are not our teachers to deal gently even with the impalpable nothings of the earth!

Therefore, as we grow older, let

us be more thankful that the circle of our Christmas associations and of the lessons that they bring, expands! Let us welcome every one of them, and summon them to take their places by the Christmas hearth.

Welcome, old aspirations, glittering creatures of an ardent fancy, to your shelter underneath the holly! We know you, and have not outlived you yet. Welcome, old projects and old loves, however fleeting, to your nooks among the steadier lights that burn around us. Welcome, all that was ever real to our hearts; and for the earnestness that made you real, thanks to Heaven! Do

7

we build no Christmas castles in the clouds now? Let our thoughts, fluttering like butterflies among these flowers of children, bear witness!

Before this boy, there stretches out a Future, brighter than we ever looked on in our old romantic time, but bright with honour and with truth. Around this little head on which the sunny curls lie heaped, the graces sport, as prettily, as airily, as when there was no scythe within the reach of Time to shear away the curls of our first-love. Upon another girl's face near it,—placider, but smiling bright,—a quiet and contented little face, we see Home fairly written. Shining from the

word, as rays shine from a star, we
see how, when our graves are old,
other hopes than ours are young;
other hearts than ours are moved;
how other ways are smoothed; how
other happiness blooms, ripens, and
decays—no, not decays, for other
homes and other bands of children,
not yet in being, nor for ages yet to
be, arise, and bloom and ripen to
the end of all.

Welcome, everything! Welcome,
alike what has been, and what never
was, and what we hope may be, to
your shelter underneath the holly,
to your places round the Christmas
fire, where what is sits openhearted.

In yonder shadow, do we see obtruding furtively upon the blaze an enemy's face? By Christmas Day we do forgive him! If the injury he has done us may admit of such companionship, let him come here and take his place. If otherwise, unhappily, let him go hence, assured that we will never injure nor accuse him!

On this day, we shut out Nothing!

"Pause," says a low voice. "Nothing? Think!"

"On Christmas Day, we will shut out from our fireside, Nothing."

"Not the shadow of a vast City where the withered leaves are lying deep?" the voice replies. "Not the shadow that darkens the whole globe? Not the shadow of the City of the Dead?"

Not even that. Of all days in the year, we will turn our faces towards that City upon Christmas Day, and from its silent hosts bring those we loved among us. City of the Dead, in the blessed name wherein we are gathered together at this time, and in the Presence that is here among us according to the promise, we will receive, and not dismiss, thy people who are dear to us!

Yes. We can look upon these children angels that alight, so solemnly, so beautifully among the living children by the fire, and can bear to think how they departed from us. Entertaining angels unawares, as the Patriarchs did, the playful children are unconscious of their guests; but we can see them— can see a radiant arm around one favourite neck, as if there were a tempting of that child away. Among the celestial figures there is one, a poor misshapen boy on earth, of a glorious beauty now, of whom his dying mother said it grieved her much to leave him here, alone, for so many years as it was likely would elapse before he came to her—being

such a little child. But he went
quickly, and was laid upon her breast,
and in her hand she leads him.

There was a gallant boy, who
fell, far away, upon a burning sand
beneath a burning sun, and said,
"Tell them at home, with my last
love, how much I could have wished
to kiss them once, but that I died
contented and had done my duty!"
Or there was another, over whom
they read the words, "Therefore
we commit his body to the deep!"
and so consigned him to the lonely
ocean and sailed on. Or there was
another who lay down to his rest
in the dark shadow of great forests,

13

and, on earth, awoke no more. O, shall they not, from sand and sea and forest, be brought home at such a time?

There was a dear girl—almost a woman — never to be one — who made a mourning Christmas in a house of joy, and went her trackless way to the silent City. Do we recollect her, worn out, faintly whispering what could not be heard, and falling into that last sleep for weariness? O, look upon her now! O, look upon her beauty, her serenity, her changeless youth, her happiness! The daughter of Jairus was recalled to life, to die; but she, more blessed, has heard the same voice, saying unto her, "Arise for ever!"

We had a friend who was our friend from early days, with whom we often pictured the changes that were to come upon our lives, and merrily imagined how we would speak, and walk, and think, and talk, when we came to be old. His destined habitation in the City of the Dead received him in his prime. Shall he be shut out from our Christmas remembrance? Would his love have so excluded us? Lost friend, lost child, lost parent, sister, brother, husband, wife, we will not so dis-

15

card you! You shall hold your cherished places in our Christmas hearts, and by our Christmas fires; and in the season of immortal hope, and on the birthday of immortal mercy, we will shut out Nothing!

The winter sun goes down over town and village; on the sea it makes a rosy path, as if the Sacred tread were fresh upon the water. A few more moments, and it sinks, and night comes on, and lights begin to sparkle in the prospect. On the hillside beyond the shapelessly diffused town, and in the quiet keeping of the trees that gird the village-steeple, remembrances are cut in stone, planted in common flowers, growing in grass, entwined with lowly brambles around many a mound of earth. In town and village, there are doors and windows closed against the weather, there are flaming logs heaped high, there are joyful faces, there is healthy music of voices. Be all ungentleness and harm excluded from the temples of the Household Gods, but be those remembrances admitted with tender encouragement! They are of the time and all its comforting and peaceful reassurances; and of the history that reunited even upon earth the living and the dead; and

17

of the broad beneficence and good-
ness that too many men have tried
to tear to narrow shreds.

CPSIA information can be obtained
at www.ICGtesting.com
Printed in the USA
BVHW040352091219
566071BV00016B/546/P

9 781163 156901